AF270663

Barbie in the 2000s

by Elizabeth Andrews

WELCOME TO DiscoverRoo!

This book is filled with videos, puzzles, games, and more! Scan the QR codes* while you read, or visit the website below to make this book pop.

popbooksonline.com/aughts

abdobooks.com

Published by Pop!, a division of ABDO, PO Box 398166, Minneapolis, Minnesota 55439. Copyright © 2025 by Abdo Consulting Group, Inc. International copyrights reserved in all countries. No part of this book may be reproduced in any form without written permission from the publisher. DiscoverRoo™ is a trademark and logo of Pop!.

Printed in the United States of America, North Mankato, Minnesota.

052024
082024

THIS BOOK CONTAINS RECYCLED MATERIALS

Cover Photo: Getty Images

Interior Photos: Getty Images, Shutterstock Images, Wikimedia, Design Bay Productions, Associated Press, MATTEL/SIPA/Newscom, Library of Congress, Alamy Stock Photo

Editor: Grace Hansen

Series Designer: Victoria Bates

Library of Congress Control Number: 2023947578

Publisher's Cataloging-in-Publication Data

Names: Andrews, Elizabeth, author.

Title: Barbie in the 2000s / by Elizabeth Andrews

Description: Minneapolis, Minnesota : Pop!, 2025 | Series: Barbie through the decades | Includes online resources and index

Identifiers: ISBN 9781098246297 (lib. bdg.) | ISBN 9781098246853 (ebook)

Subjects: LCSH: Barbie dolls--Juvenile literature. | Toys--History--Juvenile literature. | Two thousands (Decade)--Juvenile literature. | Toys--Social aspects--Juvenile literature. | Popular Culture--Juvenile literature.

Classification: DDC 688.722--dc23

*Scanning QR codes requires a web-enabled smart device with a QR code reader app and a camera.

TABLE OF Contents

CHAPTER 1
Barbie's Beginnings. 4

CHAPTER 2
A New Millennium 10

CHAPTER 3
Barbies of the 2000s. 16

CHAPTER 4
Barbie in the Real World 22

Making Connections. 30
Glossary 31
Index. 32
Online Resources 32

Barbie's Beginnings

Humans have made dolls for thousands of years. At first, dolls were made of clay, straw, or other natural materials. As the world changed, so did dolls. The toys got more detailed and exciting. In 1959, the fashion doll, Barbie, hit store shelves. The doll game was never the same.

Barbie's original striped swimsuit was inspired by fashions worn in the 1950s.

Ruth Handler was the creator of Barbie. Ruth and her husband owned the toy company Mattel Creations. Ruth noticed that children's dolls were mostly baby dolls. She believed growing girls didn't want to play with babies.

They wanted dolls that encouraged them to dream of their futures.

Ruth Handler was born in Denver, Colorado, in 1916.

Mattel released the first Barbie in 1959. She wore a black-and-white swimsuit, black high heels, white sunglasses, and gold earrings. Barbie was a teenage fashion model from Willows, Wisconsin. She cost $3. Her extra outfits ranged between $1 and $5.

The Handler family

Barbie's full name is Barbara Millicent Roberts. She was named after Ruth's daughter Barbara.

Barbie was a hit! In the first year, Mattel sold 350,000 dolls. Soon customers were asking for more. Mattel went on to create friends, dreamhouses, cars, and more than 250 careers for Barbie. Ruth was right. Children did like grown-up dolls. Their imaginations grew with Barbie!

The first Barbie appeared passive and gentle. She fit into the late 1950s female tradition of **homemaking** and beauty **trends**. Some of the first Barbies included Barbie Learns to Cook and Suburban Shopper Barbie. However, Ruth wouldn't keep Barbie in the home for long.

Suburban Shopper Barbie, 1959

CHAPTER 2

A New Millennium

The new **millennium** began on January 1, 2000! In its first decade came several global disasters. The **terrorist** attacks on September 11, 2001, changed the United States forever. President George W. Bush quickly announced the war on terror, which lasted nearly 20 years.

Some people worried about computers failing when the year changed from 1999 to 2000.

11

Several environmental disasters also took place. In 2004, a **tsunami** in the Indian Ocean hit countries in South and Southeast Asia. In 2005, Hurricane Katrina became the most expensive weather event in US history. In 2008, entire villages were destroyed by a massive earthquake in China. These disasters shaped the world.

In 2008, Barack Obama was elected President of the United States. He was the first person of color to lead the country. He ran his campaign on the promise of hope and change. Along with the White House, the whole country grew more diverse during the 2000s. California, New York, and Texas had the largest populations of people of color.

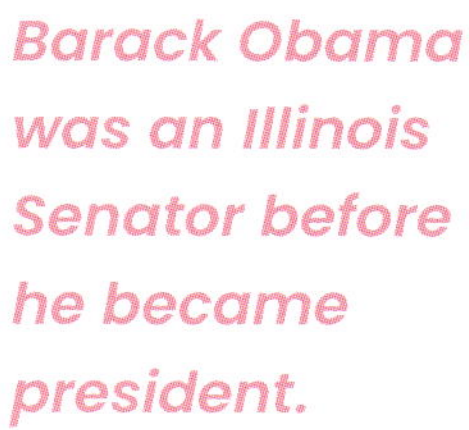

Barack Obama was an Illinois Senator before he became president.

The world was also changing. People around the globe connected as technology advanced. Internet use was at an all-time high. The invention of smart phones, such as the Blackberry and iPhone, allowed people to receive information at all times.

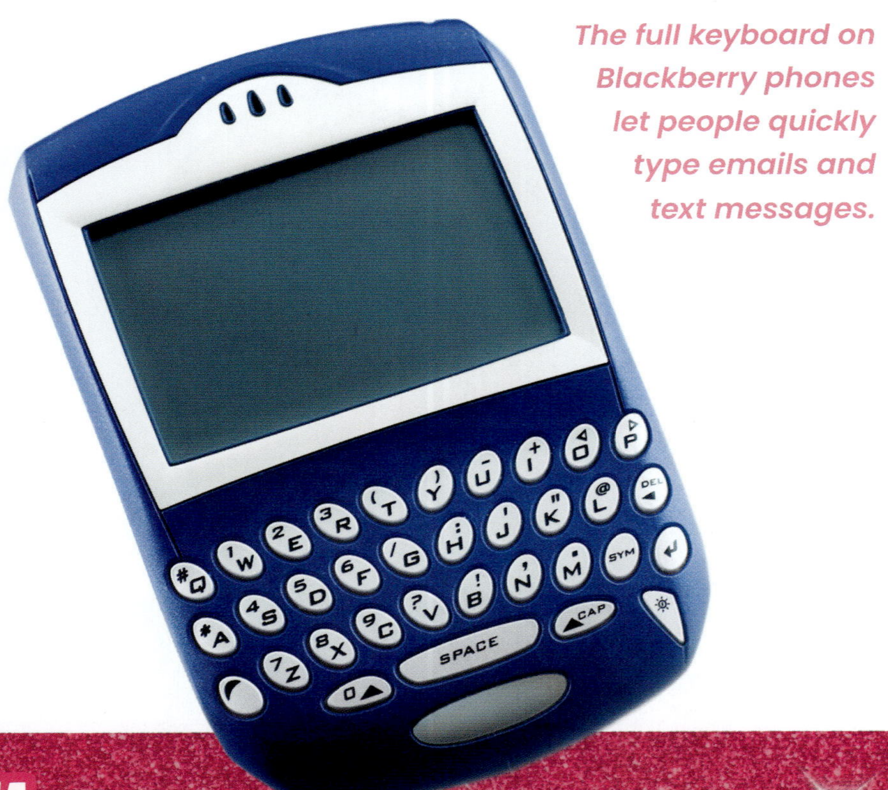

The full keyboard on Blackberry phones let people quickly type emails and text messages.

New kinds of entertainment were created during the decade as well. The first of many iPod versions was released in 2001. Video games progressed and an exciting new console called the Wii brought movement and play into people's living rooms.

Since its first season in 1999, SpongeBob SquarePants has won a record number of Kids' Choice Awards.

DID YOU KNOW? Cable television was common in many households. Channels such as Disney, Nickelodeon, and ABC Family were popular.

CHAPTER 3

Barbies of the 2000s

The 2000s brought forth a new Barbie doll mold. Jewel Girl Barbie was released in 2000. She had a belly button. Her body also looked different. Jewel Girl Barbie looked more realistic, and she could bend at the waist. This Barbie was Mattel's first move toward body **inclusivity**.

Barbie Celebration
(2000) was the first
collectible doll of
the new millennium!

When Handler invented Barbie, she knew that girls wanted to imagine their future selves when they looked at and played with their dolls. The Barbies of the 2000s had lots of hobbies. Barbie danced ballet, pet sat, rode horses, decorated nails, and more!

Barbie and Tanner, 2006

Amazing Nails Kayla, 2001

Barbie and Ken Split

After 43 years together, Barbie and Ken broke up the just before Valentine's Day in 2004. Mattel said that the couple needed to spend some time apart. There was a **rumor** the breakup happened because Ken didn't want to tie the knot.

Barbie moved on with a new man the same year. Blaine was a boogie boarder from Australia.

Cali Boy Blaine and Cali Girl Barbie, 2003

Mattel knew they could help children deepen their imaginations even more in the 2000s. Barbies from magical lands became commonplace on store shelves. Mermaids, fairies, and goddesses were just a few. Princess Barbies were everywhere with each gown more beautiful than the last.

Mattel released several Barbie collections in the 2000s. The dolls wore gowns inspired by things such as birthstones and Zodiac signs.

Barbie sales had declined in the early 2000s. So Mattel **modernized** their dolls with a line called Fashion Fever. Fashion Fever Barbies were sold in plastic tubes. They wore clothes that could be found in stores. Children could easily picture living the life they imagined for their Barbies.

Miss Diamond Barbie (April) from the Birthstone Beauties collection, 2007

CHAPTER 4

Barbie in the Real World

As the world became more **inclusive**, Mattel's dolls did too. Barbie had always had friends. In the 2000s her circle expanded to include more friends of color. Girls of all backgrounds could see dolls who looked like them doing cool things with Barbie.

Creative and stylish Nikki, who is Black, became one of Barbie's best friends. Teresa, another one of Barbie's besties, is Hispanic. She'd been around since the 1980s, but became more popular in the 2000s.

Beach Glam Nikki and Teresa, 2006

Barbie's chalkboard features the ASL sign for "I love you."

Women were closer to true equality than ever before in the new **millennium**. Barbie and her friends of the 2000s took on impactful careers. These jobs included baby doctor, American sign language (ASL) teacher, train conductor, and film producer. Children got to see their favorite Barbies in the jobs they dreamed of having!

Barbie Travel Train
with Travel Train Fun Barbie, 2001

Mattel spent the 2000s combining all kinds of new technology with Barbie. I Message Girls Barbie came out in 2004. She came with a cell phone that let kids text message with her. Mattel also began making **animated** Barbie movies. Toy sets and dolls designed like the characters in the films were popular with kids!

Barbie Video Girl (2010) is an example of the hard work Mattel put in to developing technology in the 2000s.

The first animated Barbie film was 2001's *Barbie in the Nutcracker*. Mattel continued to release one or two Barbie movies a year during the 2000s. None of the films released in theaters. Barbie fans could watch at home right away!

As internet use became common, children could dream about different parts of the world. Mattel wanted to help too! Dolls of the World – The Princess Collection was released in the 2000s. Each Barbie Princess wore elegant and traditional clothes. The back of the box had a story about the princess and her homeland.

Princess of the Navajo, 2004

Princess of the Korean Court, 2004

Barbie and her friends fit comfortably in a fast-changing world. Mattel found new and creative ways to inspire children. The next decade would see Barbie like she had never been before!

Princess of Cambodia, 2003

Princess of Ancient Mexico, 2004

Making Connections

TEXT-TO-SELF

Have you ever played with Barbie or her friends?

If so, what kind of life did you imagine for them?

If not, what kind of life would you imagine?

TEXT-TO-TEXT

Have you read any books about other toys?

What did those toys have in common with

Barbie? How were they different?

TEXT-TO-WORLD

Mattel created 21 princesses in the Dolls

of the World collection. With the help of an

adult, research one of the princesses and her

homeland. Write a few sentences about what

you learned.

Glossary

animated — describing a movie or short clip that was made using animation techniques.

homemaking — caring for a household by cooking, cleaning, and raising children.

inclusivity — the practice of including everyone. Something that includes everyone is inclusive.

millennium — a period of 1000 years.

modernize — bring up to date.

rumor — a piece of information or a story passed from one person to another without any proof that it is true.

terrorist — a person who uses violence, especially against civilians, often for political gain.

trend — a current style or preference, especially concerning clothing.

tsunami — a great sea wave produced by an undersea earthquake or volcanic eruption.

Index

American Sign Language, 25

Barbie in the Nutcracker, 27

Barbie Learns to Cook, 9

Blaine, 19

Bush, George W., 10

careers, 8, 25

dreamhouse, 8

Fashion Fever dolls, 21

Handler, Ruth, 6, 8–9, 18

I Message Girls Barbie, 26

Jewel Girl Barbie, 16

Ken, 19

Mattel, 6–8, 16, 19, 20–21, 22, 26, 27, 28–29

movies, 26, 27

Nikki, 23

Obama, Barack, 13

original Barbie, 4, 7, 9

Princess Barbies, 20

Princesses of the World, 28

Suburban Shopper Barbie, 9

technology, 14–15, 26, 28

Teresa, 23

popbooksonline.com/aughts

*Scanning QR codes requires a web-enabled smart device with a QR code reader app and a camera.